LEVEL 5

Written by: Caroline Laidlaw
Series Editor: Melanie Williams

Pearson Education Limited
Edinburgh Gate, Harlow,
Essex CM20 2JE, England
and Associated Companies throughout the world.

ISBN: 978-1-4479-4431-7

This edition first published by Pearson Education Ltd 2013
7 9 10 8
Text copyright © Pearson Education Ltd 2013

The moral rights of the author have been asserted
in accordance with the Copyright Designs and Patents Act 1988

Set in 15/19pt OT Fiendstar
Printed in China
SWTC/07

Acknowledgements
The publisher would like to thank the following for their kind permission to reproduce their photographs:
(Key: b-bottom; c-center; l-left; r-right; t-top)

A. Fong: 7br; **Alamy Images:** CountrySideCollection / Homer Sykes 25t, Bill Lyons 7tr, Gunter Marx 18tl, PhotoBliss 18cr; **Corbis:** 8-9b, Yann Arthus-Bertrand 28bl (inset), Datacraft Co., Ltd 14b, Enrique de la Osa / EFE / epa 5cl, Jorge Ferrari / epa 29cl, Jose Fuste Raga 31/f, Wolfgang Kaehler 11t, Bob Krist 28tl, Frans Lanting 13br, 20tr, 20cr, Michael Kern / Visuals Unlimited 19b, Ocean 17bc (inset), PoodlesRock 13tl, Radius Images 27cl, STR / Reuters 6t; **Fotolia.com:** a9luha 18cl, Rafael Ben-Ari 31/e, foto76 21t, joel_420 18br, Tomaz Kunst 9b (inset), Nataliya Peregudova 15br, rabbit75 31/h, rgbspace 5b, Weltenbummler 32/d; **Getty Images:** AFP 12, Ben Cranke 32/e, Dea Picture Library 21br, V. Giannella / DEA 4, Vincent Grafhorst / Foto Natura 22, M. Gréard 23bc (inset), Philip Lee Harvey 20b, Thorsten Henn 26b, Stefan Huwiler 32/b, Purestock 9tr, Tohoku Color Agency 17b, VisitBritain / Britain on View 24cl, Morio Yamamoto 15t; **Imagemore Co., Ltd:** 31/g; **Imagestate Media:** John Foxx Collection 31/c; **PhotoDisc:** Siede Preis Photography 29br; **Rex Features:** ImageBroker 27t, Richard Sowersby 24b; **Robert Harding World Imagery:** Cyrille Gibot / age fotostock 23b, Manfred Gottschalk / age fotostock 10b, Juan Carlos Munoz / age fotstock 32/a, Michael Krabs / Image Broker 17tl, Alvaro Leiva / age fotostock 7c, Luis Alberto Aldonza / age fotostock 11br, 32/f, Benjamin Rondel / age fotostock 5tr, Ragnar Sigurdsson 28b, Lucas Vallecillos / age fotostock 16; **Shutterstock.com:** Stephane Bidouze 31/d, Dariush M. 31/b, Pichugin Dmitry 31/a, Martin Fowler 25br, Nazzu 32/c; **StockFood UK:** Quentin Bacon 6b; **SuperStock:** Minden Pictures 10tl, 23tr, Nordic Photos 27bc
Cover images: Front: **Shutterstock.com:** Pablo Scapinachis

All other images © Pearson Education

In some instances we have been unable to trace the owners of copyright material,
and we would appreciate any information that would enable us to do so.

Illustrations: John Haslam and Mark Ruffle

Published by Pearson Education Ltd

For a complete list of the titles available in the Pearson English Kids Readers series, please go to www.pearsonenglishkidsreaders.com. Alternatively, write to your local Pearson Education office or to Pearson English Readers Marketing Department, Pearson Education, Edinburgh Gate, Harlow, Essex CM202JE, England.

Cuba

Cuba is the largest island in the Caribbean Sea. It is long and thin, and is 1,200 kilometers from east to west.

It has mountains, caves, tropical rain forests, plains, strange rock shapes, and beaches. Cuba has a tropical climate, so it is always hot.

There are great places in Cuba for vacations. Visitors can see unique animals and plants, and enjoy the wonderful beaches.

Cuban culture is also unique. Its music, art, dancing, and food come from all the different people who arrived in Cuba long ago.

In the warm climate, people like spending time outside. They sit and talk with their neighbors, and children play games in the street.

I'm in Cuba. Fantastic music here!

Baseball is one of the top sports in Cuba.

The main city is Havana, where more than two million Cubans live. It has some beautiful old buildings and some very old cars. The cars came from the United States as long as 70 years ago, and people still drive them.

Cuba is famous for a big festival every year in July. Young and old Cubans dance and sing, and play music in the streets.

Cuban food is a mixture of European and African cooking. There are delicious meals of beans with rice, chicken with rice, fish, salads, tropical fruit, and vegetables. Ice cream is a favorite, too.

beans

Cuban farmers grow most of the food that goes into Cuban cooking. There are wide fields of rice and sugar on the plains. Coffee grows in the mountains and also bananas, and other kinds of tropical fruit.

palm tree

One of the smallest frogs in the world lives only in Cuba. This very small animal hides on the forest floor. The frog's brown and yellow body matches the color of the leaves in this habitat.

Easter Island

Easter Island is a triangle of volcanic rock in the South Pacific Ocean. It is more than 3,000 kilometers from the nearest land of South America.

When the first people arrived on Easter Island hundreds of years ago, there were trees everywhere. These people farmed the land and cooked on wood fires. They painted pictures on rocks in caves. They also made hundreds of very large stone sculptures with big heads and bodies. The stones are 6 meters tall and very heavy, and they still stand around the island.

How did the statues get there? People probably used trees to move the stones along the ground. Today, there are no more forests, because those people from the past used all the trees. They did not plant any more.

Only a few thousand people live on Easter Island today. They love music and Polynesian dancing.

Some really scary stones here!

The Galapagos Islands

The 13 main islands and six smaller islands of Galapagos are in the South Pacific Ocean. The islands are volcanic, but only six volcanoes are still active.

Galapagos
Islands
South
America
South
Pacific
Ocean

More than 170 years ago, a scientist called Charles Darwin visited Galapagos. He was interested in the unique wildlife. He saw strange plants and animals that did not live in any other part of the world.

active volcano

The Galapagos tortoise is the biggest in the world. The female tortoise leaves her eggs in the sand, and four or five months later the babies come out. Maybe in 100 years they will be as big as their mother.

tortoise

Today, there are cats and dogs, cows, chickens, and new trees, and plants on the Galapagos Islands. They came to the islands in ships after Darwin's visit. Because of this, some of the unique animals are now endangered.

The male Blue-footed booby has a loud voice and likes dancing with female Blue-footed boobies.

Blue-footed booby

11

Marine iguana

Charles Darwin

Charles Darwin studied Galapagos Marine iguanas that swim in the sea and eat sea plants.

"Why are there dark gray Marine iguanas here?" he asked. "In other parts of the world iguanas are green."

When Galapagos iguanas climb out of the water, they are cold. They must warm up again, so they lie on black volcanic rocks in the sun. The color of their bodies helps, because the sun warms dark things more quickly.

Their dark bodies match the rocks that they lie on. In this way, they hide from other animals that could kill them. So what was the answer to Darwin's question? The bodies of Marine iguanas changed over thousands of years to match their habitat.

Marine iguanas eat salt in their sea food. When they sneeze, salt from their noses falls on their heads. They look a bit scary, but they are not dangerous.

No, these are not my feet! Do you like the color?

Hokkaido

Hokkaido, Honshu, Shikoku, and Kyushu are the four main islands of Japan. There are also 6,852 smaller islands. All the islands of Japan lie in the North Pacific Ocean, and the Sea of Japan. In this part of the world, there are many active volcanoes, and hot springs.

Hokkaido is in the north of Japan. It has mountains, lakes, active volcanoes, forests, and a beautiful coast. Shikotsu and Toya are examples of volcanic lakes with deep blue water.

Shiretoko National Park is in the northeast corner of the island. The word Shiretoko means "end of the Earth" in Japanese. It is a quiet place for brown bears that live here.

In Hokkaido, farmers produce milk and butter, which they send to other parts of Japan. Farmers also grow potatoes and other vegetables. The sea around Hokkaido is full of fish, which is an important food for Japanese people.

Japanese food is delicious.

Every winter in February, there is a snow festival in Sapporo, which is the main city of Hokkaido. The festival began in 1950 when school students produced six ice sculptures in Odori Park.

Now, there are 300 ice sculptures or more in the snow festival. People from around the world come to build bigger and better sculptures each year. They look beautiful in bright lights at night.

Honshu

Honshu Island is the largest Japanese island. Here and on the other islands of Japan, hot springs are an important part of traditional life. Many towns build hot water baths that use

the hot springs. After a visit to these baths, people feel good. Japanese monkeys like them too!

Near Nagano in Honshu, the hot springs are a great place for monkeys on cold days.

hot springs

Great weather here, but look at these silly monkeys!

Japanese culture is an interesting mixture of the old and the new. Children can go to classes to learn traditional dancing, or to play traditional drums. They can play old or new games with friends, practice sports, or spend time on hobbies.

origami

An interesting hobby is the traditional art of folding paper. It is called origami. You can make paper shapes of birds, animals, and flowers with square pieces of colored paper.

A paper penguin! What next?

Madagascar

Madagascar is a large island in the Indian Ocean, near the southeast coast of Africa. It is a beautiful place, where some of the strangest animals live. Many of them are unique to this island.

There are more than 50 different kinds of chameleon which live in the forests. They can change the color of their bodies, and they have unique eyes. One eye can turn one way, when the other eye turns the other way.

Africa

Madagascar

Indian Ocean

chameleon

Madagascar is the home of more than 50 different kinds of lemur. They live in forests which are getting smaller every year. Why? Because farmers need land for food. They cut down forests to find more space for growing food. People also want to use the wood from trees. The unique animals and plants of Madagascar are endangered because they are losing their habitats.

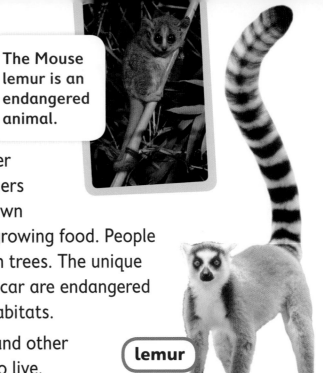

The Mouse lemur is an endangered animal.

lemur

If there are no forests, lemurs and other unique animals have nowhere to live.

Scientists can make medicines from this pretty flower.

The world needs trees and plants that could be important for science and medicine. How many are there in Madagascar? We do not know. Scientists must first find them in the rain forest. Then they must study the plants. It will be too late when the plants are no longer there.

The Elephant bird was 3 meters tall. It lived in Madagascar more than 300 years ago.

baobab tree

The baobab is one of the most useful trees for medicine. Baobabs can grow for as long as 2,000 years, and they get very big. A baobab keeps water inside its strange bottle shape. When there is no rain for months and months, the tree does not die. The Madagasy people use this water when they need it badly. It really is a tree of life.

The Madagasy call the baobab the "monkey-bread tree." Its fruit produces a traditional drink.

Madagascar has a beautiful coast with lovely beaches.

In the Andringitra National Park, visitors can walk in the mountains. They can swim in pools and climb rocks. They can also see shy lemurs that live there. There are Leaf-nosed snakes, which hide in trees, and beautiful bright blue butterflies.

Visitors must walk carefully in the wet rain forests where there could be frogs, snakes, and insects on the ground.

The Shetland Islands

Shetland is in Scotland, and it is part of the United Kingdom. There are more than a hundred islands in Shetland, but people live on only 15 of them. The Vikings from Norway arrived here more than a thousand years ago.

Shetland is a great place for wildlife. You can watch dolphins and whales near the coast. You can see millions of sea birds, too. They come because there is so much fish in the sea, and they can feed their young families.

Lerwick is the biggest town in the Shetlands, on the island of Mainland. There is a traditional fire festival here every winter. It is called Up Helly Aa.

Thousands of people carry burning torches and walk through the streets. They sing and dance, and wear Viking clothes. When it is dark, they burn a Viking boat.

Traditional festivals, music, and stories are an important part of Shetland's culture.

Take a look at this!

Iceland

Iceland is a small island in the North Atlantic Ocean, south of the Arctic Circle.

Why is Iceland called the land of fire and ice? Because it has 20 active volcanoes, and a lot of ice. There are hot springs everywhere and dangerous geysers. A geyser can shoot hot water high into the air.

Iceland has mountains, lakes, and sandy beaches. It has dark cold winters, long summer days, and millions of sea birds. There is a lot for visitors to see and do.

geyser

Icelandic horses and sheep arrived in Iceland more than one thousand years ago with the Viking people. Sheep farmers produce wool, meat, milk, butter, and cheese. Icelandic horses can live outside in winter.

The Icelandic fishing industry is very important. Iceland sells some of its fish to other countries. Traditional Icelandic cooking uses a lot of fish.

Wonderful! Ice, snow, fish, and no monkeys. Let's move to Iceland!

Surtsey

Surtsey is an Icelandic island, and it is one of the newest islands in the world. It was born in 1963 when a volcano came up from the bottom of the sea.

At first, the island did not look interesting. It was just a lot of volcanic rocks. Now, after nearly 50 years, there are plants and small animals on Surtsey. Scientists are already busy studying the new wildlife.

The Palm Jumeirah

The Gulf

Dubai

United Arab Emirates

What can people see when they are flying over Dubai in the Middle East? If there are no clouds, they can see a big palm tree in the sea near the coast. Is it a sculpture? No, it's an artificial island.

Enough traveling! It's much too hot here. I'm coming home!

The Palm Jumeirah is 5 kilometers by 5 kilometers. There are shops, movie theaters, sports centers, and 4,000 homes. Many homes have private swimming pools and beaches.

Glossary

artificial (adj) page 29   something that people make, not something which nature makes

climate (n) page 4   changes in the weather that happen through the year in a country

culture (n) page 5   the art, music, food, stories, and ideas that people have

habitat (n) page 7   a place that an animal or plant lives in

plain (n) page 4   flat land

traditional (adj) page 17   part of a people's culture

tropical (adj) page 4   hot, wet weather all the time

unique (adj) page 4   different from every other person, animal, or thing

Activity page ❶

Before You Read

❶ Think of an island which you already know,
or you would like to visit. What is the island's name?

Now look at the pictures. Which things can you find
on your island?

❷ What will you learn about islands in this book?
Say *Yes*, *No* or *I'm not sure*.

- **a** People live on every island in the world.
- **b** There are volcanoes on some islands.
- **c** There are traditional festivals on some islands.
- **d** Islands are the best places for vacations.
- **e** There are interesting animals and plants on some islands.
- **f** Some islands are artificial.

Activity page 2

After You Read

1 **Do the Island Quiz.**

    a Which islands have hot springs?

    b Which island looks like a palm tree from the air?

    c What is the name of a very big tree in Madagascar?

    d Which island has a fire festival in winter?

    e Where can you see monkeys in hot springs?

    f What is the name of the new volcanic island near Iceland?

    g Where do lemurs live?

    h Which island has a lot of old cars that people still drive?

2 **Write one sentence about each animal below.**

3 **What are the sculptures on Easter Island made of? What are the sculptures at the Hokkaido winter festival made of?**

Draw a sculpture that you would like to make.
Is it made of wood, stone, ice, chocolate, or something else? Label your picture.